CHILDREN'S EDITION

All Creation Waits

The Advent Mystery of New Beginnings

Written by **Gayle Boss**

Illustrated by **Sharon Spitz**

PARACLETE PRESS
BREWSTER, MASSACHUSETTS

"Every single creature is full of God
and is a book about God."
—Meister Eckhart

For Nathan Boss, 1934–2023
Alive always with animal wonder
—G.B.

For my beloved dog Ketem, 2011–2023
—S.S.

Contents

Author's Note 4

Introduction 6

ADVENT 1   Painted Turtle 8

ADVENT 2   Muskrat 10

ADVENT 3   Black Bear 12

ADVENT 4   Chickadee 14

ADVENT 5   Whitetail Deer 16

ADVENT 6   Honey Bee 18

ADVENT 7   Chipmunk 20

ADVENT 8   Cottontail 22

ADVENT 9   Common Loon 24

ADVENT 10   Wood Frog 26

ADVENT 11   Raccoon 28

ADVENT 12   Little Brown Bat 30

ADVENT 13   Opossum 32

ADVENT 14   Wild Turkey 34

ADVENT 15   Common Garter Snake 36

ADVENT 16   Woodchuck 38

ADVENT 17   Striped Skunk 40

ADVENT 18   Porcupine 42

ADVENT 19   Common Eastern Firefly 44

ADVENT 20   Meadow Vole 46

ADVENT 21   Eastern Fox Squirrel 48

ADVENT 22   Red Fox 50

ADVENT 23   Northern Cardinal 52

ADVENT 24   Lake Trout 54

ADVENT 25   Jesus, the Christ 56

More Animal Wonderment 58

Dear Reader,

This book is a kind of Advent calendar. The pages are numbered—Advent 1, Advent 2, Advent 3—for the days of December leading to Christmas, like the little doors on an Advent calendar. And like an Advent calendar, this book's "doors" are meant to be opened slowly, one—and only one—each day. This will not be easy. The pictures are beautiful and the animals amazing and you likely will want to rush ahead and see and read all twenty-five at once!

But in Advent, the season when sunlight is fading and cold is creeping in, all creatures know that to be well, they must wait, they must slow their usual way of doing things. You can join creatures in their Advent waiting by staying with just one animal each day. On Advent 1, sink down with Painted Turtle. On Advent 2, huddle with Muskrat. You'll be excited to see who's waiting for you each day. By December 25, you will have discovered that the animals companion us and speak to us.

I hope you enjoy getting to know and love these amazing Advent animals— our creature kin.

Gayle

To help you linger with each day's animal
there is more animal wonderment
on pages 58–64.

In late fall . . .

. . . in the world's north
      the sun glides low in the sky.
Light dims, the air cools
      signaling every living thing.
Animals know what to do
      when the season of dark and cold
      spreads over the earth.

Every creature makes changes
      to its home, its body, its habits.
Every creature makes ready to wait
      until the earth wakes again
      into the light and warmth of spring.
Waiting in the cold dark will be hard
but each creature knows
      The dark is not an end. It's a door.
      It's the way a new beginning comes.

Painted Turtle

At the bottom of the pond
Painted Turtle has buried herself.
Beneath the weight of frigid water
sealed with a layer of ice
and a skin of snow
she has stilled herself, made herself so slow
for six months she will not need to breathe.

8

If she stayed busy, not still
    the cold would kill her.
Utterly quiet in her bed of mud
    she will be safe—
        if she waits.
Waiting is her one work
    and it is not easy.
Sunk in deep stillness, she trusts
    that one day her world will warm again
    that she will breathe again

                and swim free!

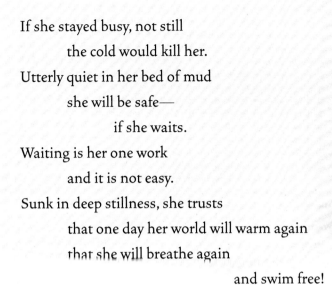

The dark is not an end. It's a door.
It's the way a new beginning comes.

9

Muskrat

Muskrat is no winter napper.

    He is an avid, frigid-water swimmer!

His thin, flat tail, like a belt on edge

    propels him deep beneath the pond's ice cap

        then up, up through a crack

            into a little hut he built of stalks and sticks.

Though his fur coat is thicker

    and his blood richer in winter

        the icy water weakens him.

In his little breathing room, he rests

    sometimes alone

        sometimes huddled with others

            sharing body heat.

Then, strong again, he dives sleek and quick

    to the pond's bottom, where fresh greens grow

        all through the season of dark and cold.

The dark is not an end. It's a door.
It's the way a new beginning comes.

11

Black Bear

Beneath some fallen tree or stump
Black Bear has dug a den
rounded to the curl of her body.
All summer, all fall, she was getting herself ready
sniffing out, licking in
berries and bugs, ants and nuts
roots and tender plants.
Eat and grow! Eat and grow! her body said
until it said, *Now, let go.*

12

Now, curled in her den, she rests
while her body turns all that food
into two tiny cubs
curled deep inside her.
Imagine her surprise in spring when she wakes
to see four shining eyes
looking back at her!

The dark is not an end. It's a door.
It's the way a new beginning comes.

13

Chickadee

A tiny acrobat swirls and twirls through the trees
        singing his name
                Chick-a-dee-dee-dee!
All fall he searched for seeds.
This one he tucked under a flap of bark
        that one in a crack of brick.
                Thousands of seeds he hid!
As he did, a kind of map grew in his brain
        the secret place of each seed marked.

Now those seeds are his only food
        and the map reminds him
                where they're hid.
Each time he eats a seed
        the seed-map shrinks.
Will the seeds and his map last
        until the ice and snow go?
Chickadee doesn't know.
        Still, he sings!

The dark is not an end. It's a door.
It's the way a new beginning comes.

15

Whitetail Deer

The wind blows cold
and Whitetail Deer—both bucks and does—
are moving, moving, moving.
The forest's strongest buck moves most
searching, searching for a certain place.
Finding it
he paws a circle in the dirt and pees
he rubs his forehead against a small tree
he bites off a branch's tip and strokes his cheek there.
He has spread his scent all across this corner of the forest.

A doe, moving past, lifts her nose.
He calls.
She calls.
Briefly, they meet.
When they part, she finds other does
and they lie close, sheltered by cedar boughs
while the fawns in their bellies grow.

16

The dark is not an end. It's a door.
It's the way a new beginning comes.

17

Honey Bee

The old oak tree is hollow and silent.
        But not empty.
Inside, twenty thousand Honey Bee sisters
        cluster together
                and shiver.
They aren't cold
        though snow swirls around their oak.
Shivering her tiny wing muscles
        each bee makes a tiny bit of heat.
Tiny bits of heat rising
        from the bodies of twenty thousand bees
        wrap a warm cloak around their queen
                who rests at their center.

As they shiver, the sisters dance
        looping, moving
                from the cooler, outside curve
                        of their cluster
                in toward the warmer core.
Each bee knows that to live through winter
        they all must dance
                and shiver together.

18

The dark is not an end. It's a door.
It's the way a new beginning comes.

19

Chipmunk

Chipmunk is good at math.
He can subtract and add
    into the thousands!
He counts nuts and seeds—
    the ones he packed in his cheeks
      and hid, above ground, below ground
        hurrying, scurrying, all summer, all fall—
          until Winter said, *Stop! Go to your tunnel!*

Curled in the earth
    he sleeps for days, for weeks.
He wakes to eat and count his seeds.
    Has another creature eaten some?
    Does he have enough?
    Should he dash to his stash above ground
        where Hawk circles and Cat prowls?
    Should he go back to sleep?
Doing math, asking questions, deep-napping—
    these habits bring Chipmunk safely to spring.

The dark is not an end. It's a door.
It's the way a new beginning comes.

21

Cottontail

Under a full moon, a stone—
    no, it's Cottontail
       quiet, still—
          until Owl hoots.
Then like a lightning bolt
          she dashes
      the zig-
zag path
      she made
         for escape
to her brush pile. Safe
    she hides through the next day
     warming herself till night comes.
Then, again, she must go out to eat.

At night, most hunters sleep.
    To others, she's invisible.
       But Owl sees.
So, before she nibbles twig tips
    she hops her paths
       packing down snow
        making them hard and fast.
    Loose snow slows her zig-zag bolt.
She packs three paths
    then settles down to eat
       quiet, still
         ready
           to leap!

The dark is not an end. It's a door.
It's the way a new beginning comes.

Common Loon

All spring, all summer, shrill calls—
   cackles and wails—
      crackle the air over northern lakes.
Common Loons cry fierce warnings:
   This nest, these chicks—mine!
Once the chicks are grown, parent loons change.
   Their snazzy feathers turn plain gray.
   Their fierce cries fade away.
   They welcome loons they once warned
      swimming together, growing strong.

When ice prickles their lakes
together they fly
many long miles
to the ocean.
There, all the strong wing feathers
that carried them so far
fall out.
Bold and loud on summer lakes
winter loons—quiet, gray, unable to fly—
can only bob on gray ocean waves
and wait.

The dark is not an end. It's a door.
It's the way a new beginning comes.

Wood Frog

Under the snow
beneath a blanket of dead leaves
in a shallow bed
lies a frog-shaped cube of ice.
Wood Frog is frozen.
But not dead.
He practiced for this.
In late fall he let nighttime's chill creep
through his body, stilling him
to ice.
When the sun warmed the morning
Wood Frog warmed
gulping, hopping!

He practiced
    freezing
        unfreezing
            freezing
                unfreezing
until winter's sun gave no heat.
He froze then and frozen will stay
    until spring warms his bed.
Then, slowly, he'll wake
    stretch his stiff frog legs
        hop to the pond
            and croak in a great frog choir:
    Glory! We're alive!

The dark is not an end. It's a door.
It's the way a new beginning comes.

27

Raccoon

Berries and worms, crayfish and chocolate cake—
    Raccoon eats nearly anything!
Each night she shows her kits
    how to sniff and listen
    how, with clever fingers
        to turn over rocks
            open locks on garbage bins.
They eat and eat
    making their backs and bottoms into blankets of fat.

When winter's wind blows cold
    they huddle inside a tree hole.
    They tuck themselves under their fat blankets
        their bodies balls of fur
        wrapped with a rope of stripey tail.
While they sleep, their backside blankets thin.
To add warm fat, they must leave their tree.
What in the frozen world will they eat?
    Nearly anything!

The dark is not an end. It's a door.
It's the way a new beginning comes.

29

Little Brown Bat

In the cave
upside down
Little Brown Bats
hang
thousands pressed together, like a great fur coat
together sharing their bodies' heat.
Winter froze the insects they eat.
Without food, the bats sleep—
a sleep so deep their hearts barely beat
their lungs barely breathe....

Except, every three weeks
    one rustles
        and jostles a neighbor
           who wakes a neighbor.
    Soon all the bats are whirling—
        peeing, pooping—
           through the cave.
All together, all winter, they sleep and wake
    until something inside them whispers
        Spring!
Hungry and thin they whoosh out
    flying their separate ways
        until another winter hurries them
        together
           back to the cave.

The dark is not an end. It's a door.
It's the way a new beginning comes.

Opossum

Shy, alone in his den, Opossum is awake.

He's not made for long sleep.

Even in biting cold, he must go out often to eat.

But without a thick fur coat

he shivers in the snow.

Worse, his ears and tail are bare.

Bit by frost, bits of them fall off.

And if he meets Fox
    Opossum is scared almost to death.
        He falls over. Can't move.
        He drools.
        His bottom leaks a green ooze
            so stinky that Fox flees!
Food and warmth Opossum often finds
    in garbage bins, sheds, and barns.
When he does, winter isn't so hard
    for shy, gentle Opossum.

The dark is not an end. It's a door.
It's the way a new beginning comes.

33

Wild Turkey

Six Wild Turkey hens run on long strong legs
      to the forest slope.
With long strong toes they shovel away shallow snow
        uncovering treasure—
           acorns, beechnuts, hickory nuts!
They cluck-purr and gobble
      nuts being the best belly-warming food possible.

They knew the nuts were here.
They also know the swamp below
      grows salad greens they can eat
        when deep snow buries their treasure.
That's why they chose this slope
      for their winter home.
For the trees, too—big firs.
When blizzards roar, the fir boughs offer shelter.
      Fluffing their feathers, they call to each other
      In this good place we'll be safe, together.

The dark is not an end. It's a door.
It's the way a new beginning comes.

Common Garter Snake

Every fall of every year
hundreds of Common Garter Snakes
slither from every direction
to a place they remember.
There, they spend warm fall days soaking up the sun
careful to eat nothing.
When winter's cold comes
they slip through a hole
down
down
to a dark den underground.

Its cool unchanging air makes it the perfect place
    to lie perfectly still and wait.
Even their empty bellies rest without food.
They only sip a bit from the den's water pools.
While they wait
    their bodies are making changes inside
        making Garter Snakes ready
           to burst up and out—
               sliding, wriggling, coiling, gliding—
                  into spring!

The dark is not an end. It's a door.
It's the way a new beginning comes.

Woodchuck

Down a long underground tunnel
　　Woodchuck sleeps.
If lifted, dropped, shaken
　　he wouldn't waken.
Sleep that deep keeps his body healthy
　　until the world turns deliciously green again.
But every few days an alarm clock inside him rings—
　　Time to poop!
Feeling good and clean he goes back to sleep.

Near winter's end his inner alarm rings
       for another reason.
Time to meet the neighbors—
       female chucks whose alarms are also ringing.
He finds their tunnels,
       they sniff and chuckle greetings.
Then he waddles home for more deep sleeping
       till spring's alarm sings
              Time for greens feasting!
              Time for companion keeping!

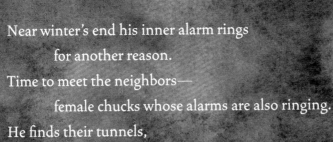

The dark is not an end. It's a door.
It's the way a new beginning comes.

Striped Skunk

Come November, Striped Skunk
    a quiet, go-it-alone soul
crawls down a hole
        where she has made her winter nest—
           and finds four skunk sisters
              resting there!
She doesn't care.
It doesn't matter who made the nest.
    What matters is togetherness.

The skunks braid themselves
    into a black and white ball
    and fall asleep.
Each needs her body's fat for warmth.
Yet all, fatter and thinner, share their heat
    throughout the ball
    so the fat of each and all lasts longer.
Through the long winter they all grow thinner.
So they curl in closer to make their furball warmer.
    Alone all summer, now they need to be together.

The dark is not an end. It's a door.
It's the way a new beginning comes.

Porcupine

At the top of a big beech tree
    rocking in the cold night wind
        Porcupine doesn't shiver.
He wears an all-body parka.
Sleet and snow slide off his prickly quills
    keeping his inner, next-to-skin fur
        warm, soft, and dry.
All night his four orange front teeth
    scrape bark into his mouth.
His one winter food, chewed wood
    scents Porcupine with sawdust perfume.

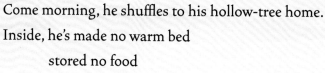

Come morning, he shuffles to his hollow-tree home.
Inside, he's made no warm bed
    stored no food
        invited no friends for a snug huddle.
He sits up, alone
    hugging himself tightly
    the wood-burning stove in his belly
        keeping him warm.

The dark is not an end. It's a door.
It's the way a new beginning comes.

43

Common Eastern Firefly

Flashing through summer nights
Firefly has disappeared from dark wintertime.
But not her light.
Before dying, she planted eggs in the earth—
eggs that glowed!—
and hatched into tiny larvae
that glowed!
Eating, growing, the larvae split their skins
and crawled out, naked, glowing.
Each grew a bigger skin
then outgrew and split it
and grew a new one again.

Eating, growing, outgrowing, glowing
    underground, firefly larvae keep crawling
        for nearly a year.
Then, each will make a cave
    and wait while her body changes.
Finally ready, she'll dig out of the cave
    and rise—on wings!—into summer's sky
        her ever-lasting fire flying.

The dark is not an end. It's a door.
It's the way a new beginning comes.

45

Meadow Vole

Beneath the wild field's snowy floor
hides a village of Meadow Voles
scurrying for food.
During summer, Meadow Vole didn't store
or eat more seeds and grass stems
to gain weight for winter warmth.
No, she chose to get thinner for winter.
So she gets cold quicker.

She has her reasons.

Thinner, she needs less food.

    That means less time scurrying

    more time in her warm nest, resting.

There, without pups to protect

    in winter, she's gentler

    willing to share her nest

        with any vole neighbor.

In the harshest weather

    when each vole is smallest and weakest

    they huddle, humming with heat

        their bodies make when they're together.

The dark is not an end. It's a door.
It's the way a new beginning comes.

Eastern Fox Squirrel

A furry flag flicks in the snow, topples
    and up pops Fox Squirrel, mouth full.
When acorns, hickory and walnuts
    fell from the trees in fall
    he gobbled his belly full
        then hid thousands more.
Nut-loving neighbors watched.

So he played nut-hiding tricks:
    Dig a hole, pretend to drop an acorn in.
    Do this again.
    Dig hole number three.
        Bury the acorn there.
            Maybe.
    Come back later, bury it somewhere new.
            Or pretend to.
For months he remembered which hole
    really hid his buried treasure.
Because Fox Squirrel doesn't want to spend winter sleeping.
    Eating nuts hidden and found
        he can keep tree-leaping!

The dark is not an end. It's a door.
It's the way a new beginning comes.

Red Fox

On paws soft as silk
　　softer than a whisper
　　　　Red Fox creeps across the field.
　　　　　　Her stomach rumbles.
All night she has hunted
　　but eaten nothing.
Now she hears squeaking under the snow—
　　　　somewhere.
She cocks one ear up
　　　　　　then the other
　　　　guessing the distance
　　　　　　to the invisible squeaker.

She looks for a shadow—
　　one inside her eye.
She turns until she sees that shadow hover over
　　　　where her ears say the squeaker sits.
　　　　The shadow shows exactly how far to it.
Rearing on her back legs
　　Red Fox leaps in a perfect curve
　　　　then plunges into the snow headfirst.
Quickly upright again
　　　　she gulps
　　finally fed.

The dark is not an end. It's a door.
It's the way a new beginning comes.

Northern Cardinal

When winter's world is mostly gray
  Northern Cardinal blazes, a scarlet flame.
In fall, he devoured red-colored fruits
   so his new feathers grew in redder.
     Females like redder males better.
Now, winter gives him only seeds.
   He's careful how many he eats.

He needs a layer of fat
   or he will grow weak and fall.
Too much fat, though
   and he will also fall.
    Fat slows his speedy escape from Hawk
     who also needs to eat.
Every winter day Cardinal asks
   Am I fat enough to stay strong?
   Thin enough to stay fast?
If the answer is yes
   come spring he'll sing
    What cheer!

The dark is not an end. It's a door.
It's the way a new beginning comes.

53

Lake Trout

As great, cold waves heave and crash
Lake Trout glides beneath
at ease.
She's returned from a very long journey.
In late fall, she felt a sudden urge—
Go home!
She swam miles and miles
to a certain pile of rocks
stacked on the lake's bottom.
A swirling communion—
a lake trout reunion—
met her there.

They swam, silver sides pressed together
until eggs fell from her body
into cracks among the rocks
hidden from hungry fish
and churning currents.
She was once an egg there, waiting to hatch.
Trusting her homeplace to shelter her own eggs
she swam away.
Now they wait.

The dark is not an end. It's a door.
It's the way a new beginning comes.

Jesus, the Christ

When the world was ready
  a girl gave birth to a baby
    in a shelter for animals.
She kissed him
  wrapped him snug
    and lay him in their manger.
The donkey, cows, and goats
  put their noses in the hay to eat
    and found a tiny human being!
They circled mother and son
  with their warm bodies
    calling softly, singing the child to sleep.

Out in the wild night fields
angels told men who cared for sheep
There is a new one born.
He will bring people peace.
When the sheep-men found the child
they saw what creation is waiting for—
a human at home with all creatures as kin.

The dark is not an end. It's a door.
It's the way a new beginning comes.

More Animal Wonderment

The creatures that share the earth with us are amazing!
And there's so much we can learn from them.

ADVENT 1 ❄ Painted Turtle

Try lying perfectly still, as Painted Turtle does. She lies still for up to six months
to stay alive and well in winter ponds. This ability can keep her alive for 30 years!
Rings on each scale of her shell show growth spurts. Wider rings show when food
was plentiful, narrow rings when food was scarce. For you, when is being still a
better choice than being busy?

ADVENT 2 ❄ Muskrat

Though Muskrat is active all winter, he needs a resting room where he can warm
up and get strong again. Where is your resting place? Muskrat can swim under the
ice for 15 minutes before he needs to rest. Sometimes he huddles in his hut with
others he doesn't like very much because he needs their body heat. Would you?

ADVENT 3 ❄ Black Bear

Black Bear listens to her body to know what to do each day and in each season.
During her summer feasting, she can double her body weight, growing from 100
pounds to 200. She loses all 100 extra pounds during winter. She's rewarded with
cubs—born while she's asleep! How does your body tell you what to do to be healthy?

ADVENT 4 ❄ Chickadee

Try singing your name as a song, like Chickadee does. If you put two nickels in your palm you'll feel how much Chickadee weighs. He needs to eat many seeds every winter day to stay alive. To remind him where he hid those seeds, his brain grows a map. Try drawing a map of your homeplace. How does your brain help you remember important things?

ADVENT 5 ❄ Whitetail Deer

Before quieting for winter, Whitetail Deer have a short period of urgent activity. Male deer (called "bucks") are so active they usually lose about one quarter of their weight, dropping from 200 to 150 pounds, for example. When do humans have urgent getting-ready times? Whitetail Deer use their bodies' scents to talk with each other. Besides using words, how do humans communicate with one another?

ADVENT 6 ❄ Honey Bee

The winter hive is full of Honey Bee sisters because Honey Bee brothers live only in summer. How would life be different if you lived with only girls or only boys during the winter? When each bee gives what she can and all the bees take turns, the whole hive is healthy. How does this happen in your "hive"?

ADVENT 7 ❄ Chipmunk

Have you ever watched a busy chipmunk? He can collect 165 acorns every day! How do you move when you have to get something done on time? How do you know, as Chipmunk does, when it's time to rest? Have someone help you count your heartbeats while resting. In winter, Chipmunk rests so deeply that his heart slows from 350 beats every minute to just four!

ADVENT 8 ❄ Cottontail

Cottontail's food is scarce in winter. To get enough vitamins, she eats her poop! To stay warm, she cools her long ears so heat doesn't leave her body through them. Why do you think Cottontail runs a zig-zag path, not a straight line, to escape from Owl? Cottontail is careful to pack down her escape paths. What are you careful about?

ADVENT 9 ❄ Common Loon

In spring and summer, Loon wears flashy feathers to catch the attention of other loons—like putting on party clothes. In winter, Loon rests from impressing others and wears plain gray. When do you want to dress up? When do you like to wear plain clothes? Loons are fierce defending their chicks and gentle when the chicks are grown. What makes you feel fierce? Gentle?

ADVENT 10 ❄ Wood Frog

Imagine yourself as a cube of ice! Wood Frog's body puts a thick syrup inside his cells to plump them so they don't collapse when frozen. And Wood Frog practices being very cold, then warming up, before his deep freeze. Are there difficult things you practice for so they're less difficult? At the end of his stressful time, Wood Frog celebrates. How do you celebrate after a difficult time?

ADVENT 11 ❄ Raccoon

Raccoon has such clever fingers that some cities have tried making locks for their garbage bins that are racoon proof—but Raccoon unlocks them! Her fingers are even more sensitive under water. What are your fingers good at? In fall, Raccoon chooses foods that will make her fat. What foods do you like better in cold weather than in warm?

ADVENT 12 ❄ Little Brown Bat

Bats lose heat faster than any animal that has a backbone. That's why bats press tightly together in their winter caves. Almost 400 Little Brown Bats would fit on this book's cover! In their winter caves, thousands sleep and wake at exactly the same time. When do you need the help of others, all working together at the same time, to do something you couldn't do alone?

ADVENT 13 ❄ Opossum

Opossum is ancient. His ancestors lived in warm jungles among dinosaurs! They traveled to cold-weather places following humans, finding some food in our gardens, fields, and trash. Still, winter is hard for Opossum. What sort of place would be hard for you to live in? Shy Opossum sometimes seems to be dead when he's scared. What do you do when you're scared?

ADVENT 14 ❄ Wild Turkey

Though they look clumsy, Wild Turkeys are triathletes! They can run faster than humans (up to 25 miles per hour), fly 55 miles per hour, and they're strong swimmers. Deep snow cripples them, though. So they choose their winter homes carefully. What makes your home special to you? How do people, like Wild Turkeys, comfort each other during hard times?

ADVENT 15 ❄ Common Garter Snake

Garter Snake slithers as far as two miles to his winter den, looking for landmarks that he remembers, like boulders and stumps, to show him the way. How do you remember the way to an important place? He must lie quietly underground with other snakes (up to 5,000 in big dens!) while his body makes changes that keep him healthy and strong. What helps your body make healthy changes?

ADVENT 16 ❄ Woodchuck

Woodchuck is exactly the same temperature as you are for most of the year. But during his winter sleep Woodchuck's body temperature can be almost as cold as snow. Every five days or so, his inner alarm wakes him to poop. When does your body wake you? In February, all woodchucks in a particular area wake at the same time. After months underground, they want to get together. When do you really want to see your friends?

ADVENT 17 ❄ Striped Skunk

Striped Skunk sometimes builds her nest in Woodchuck's tunnel. He sleeps at the tunnel's end, while she and her sisters sleep nearer the doorway. They share it peaceably. Skunk might push a bushel basket's worth of leaves into her nest to make it soft. What would you put in your nest? If you worked hard building it, how would you feel if others wanted to share your nest?

ADVENT 18 ❄ Porcupine

Tree bark and evergreen needles are Porcupine's only food in winter. What would it be like for you to eat the same food all winter—and to smell like that food?! Porcupine often lives in the same den all his life—up to 12 years. He lives there, even in winter, awake and alone. What would you miss if you lived alone?

ADVENT 19 ❄ Common Eastern Firefly

Firefly spends more than 300 days underground looking nothing like a firefly. When she hatches, she's the size of a small crumb. Using poisons in her mouth, she turns earthworms into liquid and drinks them! She grows through many skins before she's ready to fly. When has it taken you a lot of growing to be ready to do something new?

ADVENT 20 ❄ Meadow Vole

Meadow Vole is as heavy as 15 pennies. Every day she must eat as much as she weighs. How many bowls of food would equal your weight? Imagine eating that amount every day! Lighter in winter, Meadow Vole spends less time getting food. She can stay in her nest, warm with others. When is it good to stay home resting with others?

ADVENT 21 ❄ Eastern Fox Squirrel

Fox Squirrel eats two pounds of nuts every week. He remembers not only where he hides nuts, but also which kind of nut is in each hole. He hides red oak tree acorns in the most secret places and saves them for the coldest weather, because they give him more energy. How does your family get ready for difficult weather?

ADVENT 22 ❄ Red Fox

Red Fox can hear a mouse under the snow a football field away! From how far do you think you could hear a mouse? Red Fox also uses her eyes to hunt. The shadow she sees is given to her by a force inside the Earth, the magnetic field. It shows her exactly where to leap. How do the forces of nature we call "weather" affect your actions?

ADVENT 23 ❄ Northern Cardinal

Imagine being like Cardinal, so that eating blueberries turned your skin blue, or carrots turned your hair orange! He carefully measures his food and activity—not too much, not too little—to stay strong. How does your body feel when you have too much or too little food? When spring comes, Cardinal sings a song that sounds like *What cheer-cheer-cheer!* What do you sing when you're happy?

ADVENT 24 ❋ Lake Trout

In late fall, Lake Trout can't wait to go home. When do you really want to go home? When she gets home, there's a big family reunion. Lake Trout might lay as many as 15,000 tiny eggs among the rocks, eggs that wait four to five months to hatch. When do you have to wait for something you've made to be finished?

ADVENT 25 ❋ Jesus, the Christ

Jesus's first bed was in a place where animals rested. Have you ever rested with an animal? How did it feel? What song might the animals have sung to the newborn Jesus? How do you imagine it sounded? The first people to learn that Jesus was born were men who lived outside, caring for sheep. What made them happy to see him?

2024 Second Printing
2023 First Printing

All Creation Waits Children's Edition: The Advent Mystery of New Beginnings

Text copyright © 2023 by Gayle Boss

Illustrations copyright © 2023 by Sharon Spitz

ISBN 978-1-64060-828-3

The Paraclete Press name and logo (dove on cross) are trademarks of Paraclete Press

Library of Congress Cataloging-in-Publication Data
Names: Boss, Gayle, author. | Spitz, Sharon, illustrator.
Title: All creation waits : the Advent mystery of new beginnings / written
  by Gayle Boss ; illustrated by Sharon Spitz.
Description: Children's edition. | Brewster, Massachusetts : Paraclete
  Press, [2023] | Audience: Ages 6-10 | Summary: "Written specifically for
  early readers and their families, this books explores the idea that
  animals from frogs to bears wait for the hope of spring and new life in the same way
  that humans wait for the coming of Jesus, the Christ"-- Provided by publisher.
Identifiers: LCCN 2023000407 (print) | LCCN 2023000408 (ebook) | ISBN
  9781640608283 (hardcover) | ISBN 9781640608290 (epub) | ISBN
  9781640608306 (pdf)
Subjects: LCSH: Advent--Meditations--Juvenile literature. |
  Creation--Meditations--Juvenile literature.
Classification: LCC BV40 .B675 2023 (print) | LCC BV40 (ebook) | DDC
  242/.62--dc23/eng/20230221
LC record available at https://lccn.loc.gov/2023000407
LC ebook record available at https://lccn.loc.gov/2023000408

10 9 8 7 6 5 4 3 2

Published by Paraclete Press
Brewster, Massachusetts
www.paracletepress.com

Manufactured by Shenzhen Tianhong Printing Co. Ltd.
Printed March 2024, in Longang, Shenzhen, China
This product conforms to all applicable CPSIA standards.
Batch: 202403003STH